MW01233761

# CHINA DAILEY

# SHATTERED
# CHINA

THE JOURNEY FROM BROKEN TO GOLDEN

I am walking in my grandmother's prayers and my grandfather's prophecy, so this book is dedicated to my *Grandma Gloria* and *Grandpa Ralph* . . . everything I am is because of you.

"For I know the plans I have for you," declares the Lord, "plans to prosper you and not to harm you, plans to give you hope and a future."

-Jeremiah 29:11

# Table of Contents

*A Special Word* .......................................................................................vii

*Introduction* ..............................................................................................1

   Absent Parents ........................................................................................7

   Family Secrets .......................................................................................15

   Toxic Friendships ..................................................................................23

   Heartbreak .............................................................................................31

   Repairing a Shattered China ...............................................................41

   From Broken to Golden .......................................................................49

*About The Author* .....................................................................................53

# A Special Word

To my China and all Shattered China Dolls:

Your heartbreak is my heartbreak. Your heartache is my heartache. Your pain is my pain. Your suffering is my suffering. Your silent tears are my tears. Your deliverance is my deliverance. Your victory is my victory. And your joy is my joy.

*A Grandma's love,*
Gloria C. Dailey

# Introduction

F*irst off, hello! How* are you? There is nobody here but us, so feel free for once to be yourself. Can you tell me who you are? It is okay to be honest. If you do not know who you are, that is fine, too. By the time we finish, I hope you gain some insight into the person you are presently and who you need to become for your future.

Before we begin, are you ready for a change? Yes, you, the person that picked up my book. Have you been looking for something new? This book was designed to give people second chances. I know there is a fighter within you, and I need that warrior to come to the front. However, if you are not ready, put this book down because several missions must be completed before we arrive at the answer to my previous question.

This is not the same old boring narrative either. I had to be creative; because I want you . . . yes, you, the reader, to be able to cry, write, learn, and heal, if you need to, in this book. As I sit and reflect on my life and the paths that I once thought I would die on, I wanted to share my truth. There were some dark and scary moments. When I was at my lowest, I will not lie to you; it was so ugly. I never saw myself living a good life; I thought I would always suffer.

Wait, how rude am I? I get ahead of myself sometimes! I am China! It is so nice meeting you.

Everyone has been telling me to put my life story in a book, so I am finally taking the time to write it. Initially, I struggled with sharing my story because I did not know where to start. And I did not want to peel away the scabs covering those dark portions, as I did not know which parts of me I would have to face and deal with alone. I felt it was nothing out there that could save someone like me. I never thought I was even special enough for God to take notice of me.

Many people think they know me, and some may even try to judge what I share. I am merely telling *my* truth; so, before you become too opinionated, I need you to reflect on yourself and make sure I'm not a mirror reflection of your own imperfections. Taking steps to heal is never easy, but it is worth it. Have you ever wanted something so badly that you close your eyes to imagine it? I am sure some people have been in my boat.

Growing pains typically show up when it is time to grow up, and it can be exceptionally painful. It is a tough place in life that I believe every person encounters, no matter who they are, no matter how much money they have or how well they have treated people. Some people go through growing pains as children, while others aren't affected until they become adults. My growing pains began when I was a child, and oh how I hated my growing pains.

Life has a funny way of happening to us all. I think everyone is born with innocence; it's how we are raised, and the situations we go through that hardens us. People may be mistreating you; it could be your family, a lover, a career, or maybe it is you. The harder our life becomes, the more our innocence slips away. Most people are still trying to figure themselves out and heal from childhood sorrow; I know I was. I didn't have a clue about who I was . . . and was afraid to voice my pain. Does this relate to you too?

Maybe, you even settled with some things because you figured it was better to have a little of something than to have nothing at all. Well, that's pretty much how my life had been. I would find ways to escape the hands of life I was given. You may not have experienced my story, but the more I heal, the more I understood the truth that pain knows pain, and hurt people recognize hurt people.

It is normal to question things in our lives, why we look the way we do or why we suffered the way we have. I remember times I felt that I was always the problem, even when trying my best to change. Through all my questions, the biggest one I had to ask myself was: Was it Worth It?

I want you to work through thoughts and emotions, so I have provided space throughout the book to journal — a safe place where you can begin to be yourself. I hope by the end of the book; you can answer that question for yourself. Today is your chance to right your wrongs, to start your healing.

But before we get started, let me tell you a little story; maybe we are more alike than you think. However, let me go ahead and prepare you; you may want to grab a few boxes of tissues and a few bottles of wine because my story will take you on a ride.

I see my life replay, and with all the pain I faced, not having parents, being used, all that heartbreak . . . God, my heart was so shattered. To the woman I have become, was it worth it? Come talk with me, I want to share a few things with you, and I promise not to be too long. Let's see where it all started.

I'm from a small country town where you see more grandparents raising their grandchildren, as most parents are still trying to chase an opportunity that passed them by, instead of investing into their future inheritance, their children. A place where you see so much trauma and hurt. A place where you are born into generational curses reliving toxic cycles. And a place where kids raise themselves the best that they can and learn to slay their demons at an early age, lest they find themselves slayed by them.

My grandparents were well-known in the community for having a successful business and being heavily involved in church. You guessed it. I'm a PKG (preacher's grandkid).

Still, that did not take away from all the things I went through. If anything, it may have intensified my trials even more. The devil always tries to break people when we are discovering who we are and who we are meant to be. He sends "gifts" to you, which may come in the form of your heart desires. It may come in the form of a relationship, money, sometimes even a career, etc.

He is playing so unfairly, and you can't fight in a battle you are not prepared for. You will lose every time. Sometimes the pain becomes too much, and one may turn to drugs or sex to ease the pain. My soul cries for the people who feel stuck, and I am with everyone who relates to this. I am your proof life can change, even for you.

Now, let me finish with my story...

# ABSENT PARENTS

*"I will not leave you as orphans;*
*I will come to you."*
*—John 14:18*

M y *mom celebrated her* eighteenth birthday on March 15, and a couple of weeks later, on March 28, she gave birth to me. Growing up with absent parents shaped me more than I care to admit. It always made me feel like I was missing out on something. I used to wonder who I could have been —would I look different, smell different, or love different if my mom and dad had raised me?

At one point, I was angry with them and believed that I was living a cruel life where no one cared about me. I blamed them for any bad situation I was faced with. They were supposed to protect me. The more I went through, the more my heart grieved not having them. I yearned for their presence more than they will ever know. God, I needed them. I felt I was born with a disadvantage that was out of my control. Not having my mom there for certain achievements hurt me. The girls I hung with could not relate, but I felt so left out. I would see them interacting with their mothers, but I could not have mine. Soon, I realized it was not anger built up inside my heart . . . it was disappointment.

They were my first NO. Yes, you read that correctly. No matter how much I wanted them at that time, I could not have them. I have scars that cannot always be seen with the naked eye. Everyone wants their mother. It is a different love that only they can give, maybe because we are products of them, we crave only their nurture. Mothers are supposed to be our guide until we are ready to apply all that has been taught. I did not have that. I am not the first, nor will I be the last whose mother was not there.

A mother can be present yet absent. So, to any mothers reading my book, knowing that you are that mother who has not been focusing on your children as you should, correct it today. I know I still love mine, no matter how tough I may act towards her. If you have been a bad mother, I need you to fight for your children and fix it. Apologize and mean it. This is a safe place; no one will judge you. For my sisters and brothers, who are angry, we are healing; forgive them for your peace so that you will be a better mother or father to your children one day. If your parents still choose not to be there, it has nothing to do with you.

I felt so alone, which made me hold on to things longer than I should have. I remember being counted out. I was disappointed so much that I started thinking I was a failure.

The more I studied the dynamics of human behaviors, the more I realized my parents were doing the best they could, and that is not me trying to make an excuse for them. The truth is, we all have choices that we must give an account for. Their choice not to be there for me greatly affected some of the choices I made when I was their age. My focus and attention caused me to crave things to fill that void. I needed someone to love me, to fight for me. I was ready to escape the pain. I even used to try to imagine my life if I was born into a new family.

What I had to understand was that I could no longer suffer. I was tired of living in fear because of the rejection from my parents. My parents were young when they had me, and they were still trying to learn who *they* were. I realized that I could no longer punish them for my childhood, especially when I reflect on my mistakes at that same age.

During the time I was making bad mistakes, I did not view them as bad . . . I believed that I was doing the best I could. Once I understood that concept, I forgave them. That forgiveness was more for me, not them. See, the older and more mature I became, I understood that I could hold them accountable because now they knew better; however, only they could choose to be in my life. I was past forcing anything in my life, whether it was them, a man, or even a ponytail (hopefully, that made you laugh).

# A Reflection

What would you say to the old you and the future you? Remember, be you . . . express yourself, put it in a safe place so you can read it later in the future!

_____

_____

_____

_____

_____

_____

_____

_____

_____

_____

_____

_____

_____

_____

_____

_____

# FAMILY SECRETS

> *"There is nothing concealed that will not be disclosed, or hidden that will not be made known."*
> —Luke 12:2

*I thought that God had* cursed me with having this body. You know — that grown woman shape at a young age? I felt this way because when I was younger, I was molested by my sister's father. Whew, I can't believe I am finally sharing this with the world. Imagine holding that secret in.

He hurt me so badly, guys; he made me feel so low and dirty. I hated when my mom would go to work and leave my middle sister and me alone with him. He would wait for my sister to fall asleep, and then he would wake me up and touch me, making me do things that no child had any business doing. I still remember every single place he touched or put his mouth on.

Every time he got away with touching me or making me feel on him, a piece of China was lost. I had all these emotions running through me that I could not process at my young age. It would be years later when I transferred to North Carolina A&T in Greensboro, NC, that I learned all the damaging effects this man had and all the precious pieces he had taken from me. It took God sending me to become a social worker, to understand broken China. Now mind you, I have been suffering since I was a child, and my healing did not start until I became an adult.

At that moment, at around twenty years old, I truly understood what good self-esteem was and that I realized mine was shattered. I hated every detail about me; I felt people could see some sign hanging from me telling them I was different. Even then, I honestly hated being shapely. Can you imagine the pain I felt as I matured and learned the names of the things he made me do or that he did to me? So many silent tears. I lost my virginity to a grown man without him having my consent. It was not a scene from a fairytale or my being in love. I was not prepared, but mostly, it was not my choice as he had forcibly taken it, and I hated that shit. I viewed sex differently; it was nothing special to me. In my mind, I was already tarnished.

The crazy part is running into my father years later and hearing him tell me why he was not there for me. He told me he was working at a factory at the time and he made a new friend. He said, "China, me and my new friend have something in common, and you will not believe this"... Of course, I told him to continue, but I was not prepared for what he said next. He became friends with my sister's father, the same man who molested me, his daughter. Life can be so cruel at times.

If someone was a coward and touched you or took parts of you — get up, we will not let them win. Your body is yours. I do not care if it was your father, a family friend, a church member, or even a lover. If you need to report it, do so. Today, I want us to take our lives back from whoever harmed us, Shame on them for trying to destroy someone so special. I could not believe my abuser tried to steal the sparkle from my eyes. If this has ever happened to you, know that I am here to support you. It is my belief that every trifling person who has attempted to destroy someone will give an account for all of the damage they have caused.

Now, let me change things up just a bit. If you have witnessed someone taking advantage of someone you birthed or know, you have a duty to put an end to it. I hate to see people get hurt, but especially kids, because they cannot defend themselves. If a child brings a worry or discomfort to your attention, as an adult, it is your job to address it and get them the help they need. Do not allow them to grow up thinking you did not care. A lack of action by an adult often causes the child to build a shell around their heart and makes them think that it is okay for people to get away with hurting them. It is not okay.

It is time for people to stop making excuses for people's transgressions, stating they were drunk or on drugs when they committed disturbing offenses like inappropriately touching or abusing kids. The thought of exposing a child to danger because someone cannot control their behavior sickens me. If the offender is an alcoholic or drug addict, kick them out of the house until they can be in their right mind. They do not deserve to be around kids if they are unstable. They need to be in a recovery center.

My change came when I realized I could no longer live in a shell. I am more than others nasty traits or ways. I shared this with you because I am NOT A VICTIM. That would give that coward too much power over my life. I don't believe there is anyone more powerful than God. I was no longer willing to walk with my head down and be ashamed because he robbed me. I was never created in my offender's image, so I was determined to heal. This process was challenging because a lot of people did not understand that the biggest thing he touched was my mind. I started having thoughts and urges that were out of my control. I was young and could not understand why I had to go through this.

I was so ashamed, and I thought I was so ugly. At one point, I did not know how to make myself pretty. Food then became my comfort, my lover, my best friend, because I did not know how to help myself. (Grab yourself some tissues. I just did; not because I am sad but because I made it.) Now let me wipe these tears... I am still here with you. Trust me, please. If this happened to you and you are reading this, I am so sorry, and if I can, let me send you some strength because I need you to survive. I believe in you so much; I know you have what it takes.

Parts of this may get ugly. See, this is China talking to you, and I am not trying to make it sound good or paint a pretty picture that looks good. I want you to survive, but mostly I want you to heal. I love you so much. Whew, I promise I am not a cry baby, but I wrote this from the deepest part of my heart.

## A Reflection

Listen, we all have experienced some type of disappointment. Even if what I have shared is not your story, you have also experienced a degree of pain and disappointment. Share it in the space provided below.

_____

_____

_____

_____

_____

_____

_____

_____

_____

_____

_____

# TOXIC FRIENDSHIPS

> *"A friend loves at all times,*
> *and a brother is born for adversity."*
> *—Proverbs 17:7*

Growing up while being dark-skinned was no privilege. When I was younger, I remember getting teased for being so dark. It did not help that my friends were always "lighter-skinned" than me. I got picked on so much that I vowed to change my ways — no more being nice. And that's when building up a wall all began.

I thought my grandparents were rich, so one day, after being picked on relentlessly by some of my peers, I came home and begged my grandparents to buy something or do something to make me lighter. I felt that if I could change my skin color, I would be pretty and attractive to boys — as if having lighter skin was the cure to most of my problems.

That kind of teasing from my childhood shaped a flawed concept, and I started letting others' images of how I should look affect me. I started thinking that if I could change how I looked, my life would be better. Life does not work like that. I believe that everyone should be themselves, and if a person looks deep enough, their strongest traits will start to appear. Your beauty is how you view yourself. Please choose your friends wisely; it does make a difference. Do not befriend people who go along with the jokes or laugh at your insecurities. No real friend will laugh at things that make you uncomfortable. If your friend will not stand up for you, then it is simple, they are not your friend.

I have always viewed friendships as essential. The real friends I had, became family over time. Did you know you can have soul ties with friends too? Stop letting people take advantage of you. I do not care how long you have been in that friendship; you owe it to yourself to sever negative ties. I have witnessed how certain people got away with doing others wrong simply because of "who they were." I started to see that for some, life was about popularity.

Listen, God has a way of exposing people. I realized people enjoyed me more when I was in "need" of them. The more I healed, the more I started to see them disappear from my life. I stopped trying to understand why, out of ALL people, they would treat me this way. At one point, I wanted to get even. My mind could not grasp how I had consistently been there through all their problems — the ONLY person they could trust with their deepest secrets, those same secrets that I have kept to this very day — yet, I was the person to receive their disrespect.

I recall when two of my friends told me that what I went through was too much for them (imagine how I felt living through it). It hurt me that they viewed me that way because I was there for them, but they couldn't be there for me. I could not control the events that happened to me, even though I tried. Some days life was hard, I was tired, and I felt stuck.

I remember God told me, "China, you do not have to suffer for the sake of others anymore. You can't make anyone love you". I realized this, and I had to love them from a distance. See, I was never the friend that had money; I was the friend with no parents, I was the friend teaching me, I was the friend who was bigger, I was the friend who was dying while trying to hold on to a life that gave up on me since the day I came in this world, yet I gave each of them the best gift I had. I gave them love with no judgment, even though they hurt me.

I have always watched from the background. I could not let them eat at my table, but I would send bread to theirs without expecting anything back whenever I saw them hurting. I did this in the form of prayer. There were signs that they had served their purpose and time in my life. I had to learn to watch and listen and then let them go. It was hard to do.

To have a friend is to be a friend. I believe that you find out who your true friends are once you have nothing to give. It was during those moments that I came to see what people honestly thought of me. If you are reading this and you have been that toxic person . . . *get it together.* Apologize and decide whether you want to lose the people who care for you. As long as you are living, you can correct your wrongs.

No one wants to spend life alone; we all need someone. It gets lonely — and trust me, your hurt shows when you hurt good people.

## A Reflection

There is a saying, "If you knew better, you would do better." So, now that you know better are you willing to make the changes needed? Write about what that looks like for you.

_____

_____

_____

_____

_____

_____

_____

_____

_____

# HEARTBREAK

> *"And we know that in all things God works for the good of those who love him, who have been called according to his purpose."*
> *—Romans 8:28*

I *was nervous and excited* when I started college in August of 2012. Moreover, I was also afraid because, by this time, I was fully aware of how deeply damaged I was. Despite this, I was so ready to leave the "252" (my hometown area code) since, in my opinion, I stuck out like a sore thumb. I did not relate to those people, and they did not relate to me. I no longer wanted to live in a place where people could not see the pain I was living through.

And in my mind, in this new space, I could be whoever I wanted to be. I did not have to be broken China, or China without parents, or China who could not dress. I could share the parts of my life I wanted to. As we all know, life does not work like that.

I encourage everyone to try college. Yes, the education is good, but the best knowledge college gives is understanding yourself — the test of your strength and will to survive. If you've never had to live in death, thank God, baby, I mean thank him from the deepest part of you. I fell in love my freshmen year. Your girl was deep in love; I would have moved mountains for him. I had NO business dating him.

I was too broken. (but let me finish; we will get back to this point). I wanted someone to love me so much; this mindset caused me to pour too much of myself into a bad relationship. I remember when we first started dating, I told him I did not have a lot of money, and I was not the prettiest, but I could give him a love he had never experienced — a love that allowed him to grow, a love where I did not tally wrongs, and a love that gave pure acceptance. The whole time I was giving him something I so desperately longed for, that type of love that needed to be invested into me. This is where my obsession with making others happier than myself began because I wanted to save people from pain.

I was so ready to have someone notice me. I wanted a boyfriend so bad that I ignored all the signs. Have you ever experienced that before? Don't try to act like we haven't all wanted someone to notice us other than family members whose opinion doesn't count! Plus, in my mind, this was the first guy that gave me attention, so I had to hold on to him. I was not letting him go without a fight. Was he a bad man? I would not say he was, but he was all bad for me.

Guys, nobody should be able to drag you emotionally. I remember the days I felt like I was begging him to give me love, and he refused. Yes, he gave me nice gifts, but what I wanted from him he could not give. But I stayed because I had hope that he could change for me. After all, even though I was shattered, I knew one day my life would change. However, he repeatedly showed me that I was not the person for him. I wanted him to be my everything so intensely that I lost a part of me each time I held on to him. By the time I realized it, I no longer had an image. I would look in the mirror, and I hated the person I saw. I wondered, was I too ugly? Was I too broken? Love should not make you lose yourself, nor should it make you suffer, especially in silence.

Always be careful who you give yourself to. Love is so powerful, yet much like fine china, it is fragile. If you fall for the wrong person, you become lost in them. You see the hurt they are causing, but you no longer know how to escape from it. Pay attention to how people talk to you. I saw myself as a weak girl who had been fighting for someone to hold on to me, even though every sign showed me he was ready to let go. I begged him to see me, believing that he was the love I needed. Or did I come in chasing after things that people in love should naturally give to you, like their affection, time, and attention? That is why very often, some victims stay with their abuser.

I had dreams, and I had no intentions of starting my schooling over. I was supposed to go to law school in 2016 once I graduated from St. Aug., but I had just found out I had to start over and would not graduate until 2018. I did not understand why God sent me back to North Carolina A&T when I was on track to graduate in 2016 from Saint Aug. I was so mad at God; hadn't I suffered enough?

At that point in my life, I no longer knew how to trust God; I had suffered too much in my life. Why did my life always have to be difficult? Then on top of that, the guy I was in love with left me and got with the same girl he told me not to worry about. I experienced a functional heartbreak — because I still helped people (who could not see me suffering), all while my heart was ripping into shreds, and I did not know how to stop my own pain.

I thought God had left me. We were friends when I was a child, and I would tell Him the people who hurt me. But it seems that the more I was hurt, the more my vision of him became blurry.

Then one day, it was as if every prayer I heard spoken over me came back. I now know why God sent me back to North Carolina A&T. God loved me so much he sent me back to where my grandparents were established, to mold me as he shaped them. He was ready for me to lean on him more fully. It was like I felt my grandparent's strength. Although I felt pain, my head was slowly starting to lift; my back became straighter. I was on the battlefield, and God created me to be a warrior. It was during those days at A&T that I saw myself defeating all that tried to kill me; I refused to die, so I fought, and every time life thought it had me. I started learning and loving me.

I started to be swift to hear and slow to speak. I knelt before the Lord and said I don't know how you can use a person like me. Indeed, I am not worthy of your forgiveness, God; I need you though, I can't continue to suffer because it hurts too bad, and I would rather die. Then I realized death was too easy. I was a Queen in every sense of the word, so I asked the Lord to come to me and make me strong, but He showed me that I was already strong. He never left me . . . I had left Him, but thankfully, I was raised by the best, Gloria and Ralph Dailey. They fasted for my survival, even when I hurt them. Lord knows I love my remarkable, black excellence, strong-willed, determined, trustworthy, Leaders, resilient, God-fearing grandparents for never giving up on me.

At this moment, I am playing gospel music because someone reading this may have been praying for a sign of what to do. This is your confirmation. Let it go, let it go; get up, and let it go right now. Life can't continue to take the best of you. You are not this weak person created to lie down and accept things. They are not your parents; they did not give life to you, so leave them. You do not have to have everything figured out.

Everyone has a weakness. I have learned that people have different faces for different people. When a cop comes, they clean their act up, or maybe when they see other people, they try to act like a good person. I am praying for you as I type. I have been praying that this book reaches the person it needs to. I am rooting for you, love, that all your needs will be met. I am trusting God for the both of us just in case you are not there yet.

## A Reflection

Has anybody ever made you feel that weak? It is time for you to get it out of your system and disconnect that soul tie. Take a moment to reflect — and then release — those feelings now so that you can move on.

_____

_____

_____

_____

_____

_____

_____

_____

_____

_____

_____

_____

# REPAIRING A SHATTERED CHINA

> *"but those who hope in the LORD will renew their strength. They will soar on wings like eagles; they will run and not grow weary, they will walk and not be faint."*
>
> —Isaiah 40:31

My *demons did not* fully affect me until I was off by myself, no guide, no family, just China. It was as if every emotion I'd ever thrown under the rug came to attack me at the same time. I experienced feelings that I had never felt and cried enough tears to last a lifetime. My adult pain did not compare to my childhood sorrow. No one told me my childhood pain would grow up too, so the pain I felt at six was now eighteen. I should have been healed, but once again, life is not that simple.

I became very dark. I yearned for someone to love me other than my grandparents. I went about blaming and embracing every hurt I had felt from my childhood. I started questioning God again. How could he have created me, yet I suffer so much? I was so hurt and so broken within. The only way I could ask for help was by being overly aggressive. My pain made me protect myself in ways that were harmful to me.

People always said I was so loud, but I had to be to drown out other voices. There came the point in my life when I allowed myself to embrace falling apart. It is so hard to heal when everyone has an opinion of you. I had to be shaped in my own image. I had to grow to stop letting people's words shape who they thought I should be or how I should act. I would get so angry because it seemed so easy for them to judge looking in from the outside. But the people I was hanging with at the time wouldn't have lasted twelve hours in my shoes.

Never allow people to shape your inner strength. Find your voice. Most days, I laughed until I cried. I was hurt, and I could not control it. People had taken so many parts of me; I was used mentally, abused physically, and neglected emotionally. I gave myself away to everybody but God. I remember praying to God the night before I made a significant change in my life. I had to get my confidence back. I had to learn to live. I cut all my hair off, so I could be a natural me. I had already spent far too much time wanting to be someone else.

Feeling lonely was my most demanding test. Looking for love and wanting it but feeling like I couldn't receive it was hard. There were many days I struggled, wondering if I was enough. I heard so many people always telling me I was a good person, but why did I feel I had nothing to show for it? I would look in the mirror and get lost in my thoughts, trying to process why I was so furious with how others perceived me. Looking for these feelings put me in places where I had no choice but to grow.

I learned that no matter how much you change yourself, people will always find something to critique. I could no longer be held captive to this unhealthy mindset. I needed to feel love; that is what my mind kept saying. The mind is so powerful. You can start thinking something so long and so much until you feel you need it.

I don't know if I even gave people a chance to reject me before rejecting myself. I went through a stage when I believed I was meant to heal others, to help them reach goals that I felt even I could not master. I tried not to stand out, but my pain made me angry. I tried to be cheerful, but my truth is I had been unhappy for some time. There was no map telling me where to go, and I felt like life was passing me by. And every time I tried to touch the things I wanted, I couldn't grasp them.

I was never taught of the strength of loving me. I never knew I could be addicted to loving myself. What I once looked for in other people, I started craving from within myself. It was as if once my eyes were opened, the only image I was infatuated with was me. I loved my curves because they represented the different roads I had encountered. I loved the darkness of my skin, it reminded me of a smooth summer night, and you could see stars reflected from me if you looked deep enough. I loved the shortness of my hair; I felt so in tune with the natural and raw state of being a woman. I loved my lips because they could articulate my inner thoughts and be gentle if needed, and don't get me started on my smile; it could comfort the darkest person.

Through my years of living, I have strived to be better. You see, I know life isn't promised, so for the days I am blessed with, I will take chances. I will love, I will not be a victim because it takes too much of me to stay in my pain. My healing began because during the times I thought God hated me, I actually saw more of his favor.

Life shapes the best of us, and I am more than a survivor. I am a healer, I am a teacher, I am a future wife and mother, I am a believer, but most importantly, I am China S. Dailey. When my grandfather told me I was *becoming* me, I was confused, but Ralph always had a way of seeing me before I did. In 2020, my grandma taught me something that will stick with me forever: People can't give you what they don't have, and they can't accept what they have never experienced. God, I love my grandparents.

So, back to my original question; Was it worth it?

Yes, it was worth it. I never thought I would say this, but, the woman I have become, the knowledge that I gained about myself was worth every single tear I have shed. You read that correctly. If I had to go through every detail again — the molestation, not having my parents, the low self-esteem, or the pain in general, I would. I am glad that I made it through, so I can help others. I was created through the fire.

My voice was established because I kept going. I am beautiful because when ugly things happened to me, I never let it determine how I interacted with others. To have suffered in the way that I have, I am glad that God trusted me to assist people who may be going through what I have already come through; or maybe suffering some other traumatic pain. I grew, and no one ever told me life would be easy because it is not. I have met so many people along my life journey, and to each of you, I have encountered, even if your stay was short, I cherished it.

I made it, and so have you.

The fact that you are reading these words shows me the strength that is in you. I am so proud of you; you kept fighting. Wow, we are making it. Every detail of my life was worth it; my days are brighter because I am a survivor. I made it out of affliction. One question, my friend, was it worth it for you?

*A Reflection*

How has the pain or heartache you have experienced helped you become someone you can be proud of?

_____

_____

_____

# From Broken
# to Golden

> *"The Spirit of the Lord is on me, because he has anointed me to proclaim good news to the poor. He has sent me to proclaim freedom for the prisoners and recovery of sight for the blind, to set the oppressed free." –Luke 4:18*

A *s you see,* I needed to share my story because some people are hurting beyond the natural eye: your co-workers, your children, or even you, the person reading this. Always be mindful of how you treat others because you never know who is going through.

When I wrote this, I was crying . . . but not because of sadness, but because my life is replaying and I was never last. It just took me time to grow to this stage. I now realize that as humans, we will always be faced with something and that it is normal to be disappointed, but it is also normal to experience joy. I pray that everyone who reads my story reflects on their story. Why? Because I want you to heal. I don't care who you use to be . . . you owe it to yourself to become whole.

Pick yourself up, for today is your new beginning. Do not wait to get your second chance because I need you to inspire someone too. You are more than your mistakes. You are more than your fears, but most importantly, you are more than your pain.

Some people spend most of their lives waiting for other people to confirm the change they see in them. Know that people can see your difference and will not acknowledge it. Do not become discouraged about this; we must move from needing others' validation of who we are.

The truth is, I understand why people turn to drugs or commit suicide. Do not judge people when they become that low. I have been at low places in my life, where the darkness runs so deep you feel no one can help you. Even though I have been low in life, as strong as I was, there were days I thought I was losing my mind. I even tried therapy, only to end up counseling my therapist at a young age. Imagine that. I would share with them parts that broke me, and they would cry. I remember getting angry because if they cried just by hearing my story, then the affliction I was daily walking through was by far even greater.

I need you to live; I honestly care for each of you from the bottom of my heart. Remember, we are healing together; yes, you the person who dared to keep reading. Grab my hand; I do not have plans of leaving you alone. Now, do we relate? I hope the tears you may have shed made you feel a little lighter. Would you like to learn how to go about loving yourself and finding your voice?

Get up right now and go to a mirror. Now, take a deep breath. You have this. Look at the reflection in your eyes. This is not about feeling sorry for yourself. Embrace yourself — look at the flaws, the secrets you have been hiding, and tell yourself, I am not my mistakes. I deserve love from me the way I have desired it from others.

Each day, I will try for us. I will never tell you to do something that I have not tried for myself. I will never expect you to have a strength that I have not mastered. I believe in you, yes, YOU!

This is the end for now. Not your typical end but more of a see you later. I will be back for part two! I have enjoyed telling you how I became *golden* China. I hope you learned that I made mistakes, I hurt, I was a victim, but I needed something new. The newness I required was in me all along. Every end is not the end but the beginning of something great. I thank you for opening wounds you may have thought were healed. The fact that you had the courage to finish my book, I know you are ready to take the steps needed to continue to strive to be all you can be.

If I could encourage just one person, I would say, "Don't give up on God because He won't give up on you." This is why I am planting seeds in you that will become a harvest. I need you to make sure you take care of your harvest. I pray that everyone who encounters my book feels a strength you have not felt in a long time.

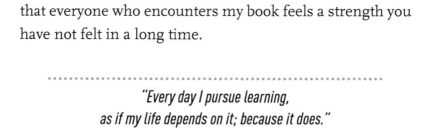

*"Every day I pursue learning,
as if my life depends on it; because it does."*

**-author unknown**

You have received knowledge; now apply it and encourage someone else to do the same. Thank you, I can't wait for us to meet up again and catch up on where we are on this journey because there are more lessons I am sure we will learn. With great love from me to you...

*China S. Dailey*